·*Cooking for Today*·

SOUPS & BROTHS

·*Cooking for Today*·

SOUPS & BROTHS

ROSEMARY WADEY

SMITHMARK

This edition published in 1996 by SMITHMARK Publishers,
a division of U.S. Media Holdings Inc.
16 East 32nd Street, New York, NY 10016.

SMITHMARK books are available for bulk purchase for sales promotion and premium use.
For details write or call the manager of special sales, SMITHMARK Publishers,
16 East 32nd Street, New York, NY 10016; (212) 532-6600.

Produced by Haldane Mason, London
for
Parragon Book Service Ltd
Unit 13–17
Avonbridge Trading Estate
Atlantic Road
Avonmouth
Bristol BS11 9QD

ISBN 0-7651-9856-8

Printed in Italy

1 0 9 8 7 6 5 4 3 2 1

Acknowledgements:
Art Direction: Ron Samuels
Editor: Vicky Hanson
Series Design: Pedro & Frances Prá-Lopez/Kingfisher Design, London
Page Design: Somewhere Creative
Photography: Joff Lee
Styling: Maria Kelly
Home Economist: Rosemary Wadey

Photographs on pages 6, 18, 34, 48 and 60 reproduced by permission of
ZEFA Picture Library (UK) Ltd.

Note:
Cup measurements in this book are for American cups. Tablespoons are assumed to be 15 ml.
Unless otherwise stated, milk is assumed to be full-fat, eggs are standard size 2 and
pepper is freshly ground black pepper.

Contents

CHILLED SOUPS   *page 7*

Gazpacho 8
Vichyssoise 10
Avocado & Mint Soup 12
Spiced Apple & Apricot Soup 15
Curried Shrimp Soup 16

VEGETABLE SOUPS   *page 19*

French Onion Soup 20
Beet Soups 22
Creamed Parsnip & Tarragon Soup 24
Creamed Carrot & Cumin Soup 27
Cream of Jerusalem Artichoke Soup 28
Pumpkin Soup 30
Gardener's Broth 32

FISH SOUPS   *page 35*

Bouillabaisse 36
Moules Marinière 38
Partan Bree 41
Shrimp Gumbo 42
Smoky Haddock Soup 44
Salmon Bisque 46

CHOWDERS   *page 49*

Hollandaise-Oat Chowder 50
Curried Cod Chowder 52
Cock-a-Leekie Soup 55
Sage & Onion Chowder 56
Red Bean Chowder 58

MEAT & POULTRY SOUPS   *page 61*

Chicken & Chestnut Soup 62
Creamed Pheasant Soup 64
Consommé 66
Scotch Broth 68
Lentil & Ham Soup 70
Split Pea & Ham Soup 73
Mulligatawny Soup 74

MAKING SOUPS & BROTHS   *page 76*

Index 80

CHAPTER ONE

Chilled Soups

Of all the hundreds of types of soup, chilled soups must be the most elegant. They are most likely to be served in the summer, or at least on a warm day, and probably for some kind of entertaining, rather than just an everyday meal. Chilled soups have delicate flavors, often enhanced by a particular herb, and are usually smooth and velvety, although a little texture is often added by stirring in some chopped or grated ingredients, such as in Gazpacho (see page 8).

Vegetables, fish, shellfish, meats, poultry, and fruit all feature in chilled soups, so they can be made to suit any kind of meal and for all tastes. Chilled soups are often finished with cream, fromage frais, or yogurt, either stirred into the soup before serving or swirled or spooned on top as an attractive garnish.

On a really hot day, a little finely crushed ice can be added just before serving the soup, but don't overdo it or it will dilute the soup too much. Most recipes can double up as delicious hot soups to serve throughout the year. Good accompaniments to chilled soups are all types of warmed bread or rolls, Garlic or Herb Bread (see page 76), Biscuits (see page 77), or Melba Toast (see page 32).

Opposite: *A chilled soup is the perfect first course for a lunch "al fresco".*

STEP 1

STEP 2

STEP 3

STEP 5

GAZPACHO

This favorite Spanish soup is full of chopped and grated vegetables with a puréed tomato base, and is served with extra chopped vegetables and Garlic Croutons (see page 79).

SERVES 4

¹/₂ *small cucumber*
¹/₂ *small green bell pepper, chopped very finely*
1 lb ripe tomatoes, skinned, or 14-oz can crushed tomatoes
¹/₂ *onion, chopped coarsely*
2–3 garlic cloves, crushed
3 tbsp olive oil
2 tbsp white-wine vinegar
1–2 tbsp lemon or lime juice
2 tbsp tomato paste
scant 2 cups tomato juice
salt and pepper

TO SERVE:
chopped green bell pepper
thinly sliced onion rings
Garlic Croutons (see page 79)

1 Coarsely grate the cucumber into a bowl and add the chopped green bell pepper.

2 Blend the tomatoes, onion, and garlic in a food processor or blender, then add the oil, vinegar, lemon or lime juice, and tomato paste, and blend until smooth. Alternatively, finely chop the tomatoes and finely grate the onion, then mix both with the garlic, oil, vinegar, lemon or lime juice, and tomato paste.

3 Add the tomato mixture to the cucumber and green bell pepper and mix well, then add the tomato juice and mix again.

4 Season to taste, cover the bowl with plastic wrap and chill thoroughly – for at least 6 hours but preferably longer for the flavors to meld together.

5 Prepare the side dishes and arrange in individual bowls.

6 Ladle the soup into bowls, preferably from a soup tureen set on the table with the side dishes around it. Hand the dishes around to allow the guests to help themselves.

SERVING
SUGGESTION

Hot Garlic or Herb Bread (see page 76) makes a good accompaniment.

STEP 1

STEP 2

STEP 3

STEP 5

VICHYSSOISE

This is a classic creamy soup made from potatoes and leeks. To achieve the delicate pale color, be sure to use only the white parts of the leeks. Vichyssoise is also excellent served hot.

SERVES 4–6

3 large leeks
3 tbsp butter or margarine
1 onion, sliced thinly
3 cups chopped potatoes
3$\frac{1}{2}$ cups Chicken or Vegetable Stock (see pages 77–78)
2 tsp lemon juice
pinch grated nutmeg
$\frac{1}{4}$ tsp ground coriander
1 dried bay leaf
1 egg yolk
$\frac{2}{3}$ cup light cream
salt and white pepper
snipped chives or crisply fried and crumbled bacon to garnish

1 Trim the leeks and remove most of the green part (it can be served as a vegetable). Slice the white part of the leeks very finely.

2 Melt the butter or margarine in a saucepan and fry the leeks and onion slowly for about 5 minutes without browning, stirring from time to time.

3 Add the potatoes, stock, lemon juice, seasoning, nutmeg, coriander, and bay leaf to the pan and bring to a boil. Cover and simmer for about 30 minutes until all the vegetables are very soft.

4 Cool the soup a little and discard the bay leaf, then press it through a strainer or blend in a food processor or blender until smooth. Pour into a clean pan.

5 Blend the egg yolk into the cream, add a little of the soup to the mixture and then whisk it all back into the soup and reheat without boiling. Adjust seasoning to taste. Cool and chill thoroughly.

6 Serve the soup sprinkled with snipped chives or crisply fried and crumbled bacon.

VARIATION

To serve the soup hot, add the thinly sliced green part of the leeks after straining or puréeing, then simmer for 5–10 minutes longer until tender. Add just the cream (omit the egg yolk) and reheat gently.

AVOCADO & MINT SOUP

A rich and creamy, pale green soup made with avocados and enhanced by a touch of chopped mint. Serve chilled in summer or hot in winter.

STEP 2

STEP 3

STEP 4

STEP 5

SERVES 4–6

3 tbsp butter or margarine
6 scallions, sliced
1 garlic clove, crushed
$^{1}/_{4}$ cup all-purpose flour
$2^{1}/_{2}$ cups Chicken Stock (see page 77)
2 ripe avocados
2–3 tsp lemon juice
good pinch grated lemon rind
$^{2}/_{3}$ cup milk
$^{2}/_{3}$ cup light cream
1–$1^{1}/_{2}$ tbsp chopped fresh mint
salt and pepper
sprigs of fresh mint to garnish

MINTED GARLIC BREAD:
$^{1}/_{2}$ cup butter
1–2 tbsp chopped fresh mint
1–2 garlic cloves, crushed
1 wholewheat or white French stick

1 Melt the butter or margarine in a large saucepan, add the scallions and garlic and fry gently for about 3 minutes, stirring frequently, until soft but not colored.

2 Stir in the flour and cook for 1 minute or so longer. Gradually stir in the stock, then bring to a boil. Leave to simmer while preparing the avocados.

3 Peel the avocados, discard the seeds and chop coarsely. Add to the soup with the lemon juice and rind and seasoning. Cover and simmer for about 10 minutes until tender.

4 Cool the soup slightly, then press it through a strainer or blend in a food processor or blender until smooth. Pour into a bowl.

5 Stir in the milk and cream, and adjust the seasoning, then stir in the mint. Cover and chill thoroughly.

6 To make the minted garlic bread, soften the butter and beat in the mint and garlic. Cut the loaf into slanting slices but leave a hinge on the bottom crust. Spread each slice with the butter and reassemble the loaf. Wrap in foil and place in a preheated oven at 350°F for about 15 minutes.

7 Serve the soup garnished with a sprig of mint and accompanied by the minted garlic bread.

SPICED APPLE & APRICOT SOUP

This delicately flavored fruit soup is spiced with ginger and allspice, and finished with a swirl of sour cream. Serve it well chilled on a warm summer's day.

STEP 1

SERVES 4–6

²/₃ cup dried apricots, soaked overnight, or
*   no-need-to-soak dried apricots*
1 lb eating apples, peeled, cored, and chopped
1 small onion, chopped
1 tbsp lemon or lime juice
3 cups Chicken Stock (see page 77)
²/₃ cup dry white wine
¹/₄ tsp ground ginger
good pinch ground allspice
salt and pepper

TO GARNISH:
4–6 tbsp sour cream or plain yogurt
little ground ginger or ground allspice

1 Drain the apricots, if necessary, and chop.

2 Put the apricots in a saucepan and add the apples, onion, lemon or lime juice, and stock. Stir to mix together.

3 Bring to a boil, then cover and simmer for about 20 minutes until all the fruit is soft and broken down.

4 Leave the soup to cool a little, then press it through a strainer or blend in a food processor or blender until smooth. Pour the soup into a clean pan.

STEP 2

5 Add the wine and spices and season to taste. Bring back to a boil, then leave to cool. If too thick, add a little more stock or water and then chill thoroughly.

6 To serve, put a spoonful of sour cream or plain yogurt on top of each portion and lightly dust with ginger or allspice.

STEP 4

FRUIT SOUPS

Other fruits can be combined with apples to make fruit soups — try raspberries, blackberries, black currants or cherries. If the fruits have a lot of pips or pits, the soup should be strained after puréeing.

STEP 5

STEP 1

STEP 2

STEP 3

STEP 5

CURRIED SHRIMP SOUP

This soup is only lightly spiced with curry so the flavor of the shrimp is not overpowered. The addition of almonds and coconut adds an exotic touch.

SERVES 4

2 tbsp finely ground blanched almonds
2 tbsp unsweetened shredded coconut
²/₃ cup boiling water
¹/₄ cup butter or margarine
1 onion, chopped very finely
2 celery stalks, chopped very finely
¹/₄ cup all-purpose flour
1¹/₂ tsp medium hot curry powder
2¹/₂ cups Fish or Vegetable Stock (see pages 77–8)
2 tsp lemon or lime juice
3–4 drops hot-pepper sauce
1 dried bay leaf
¹/₂–¹/₃ cup peeled shrimp, thawed if frozen
1¹/₄ cups milk
4–6 tbsp heavy cream
salt and pepper

TO GARNISH:
4 whole shrimp
chopped fresh parsley

1 Put the almonds and coconut into a bowl. Pour in the water, mix well, and leave until cold. Strain, pushing down firmly with a potato masher or the back of a spoon, and reserve the liquid.

2 Melt the butter or margarine in a large saucepan. Add the onion and celery and fry slowly for 3–4 minutes until soft but not colored.

3 Stir in the flour and curry powder and cook for 2 minutes, stirring, then add the stock and coconut liquid and bring to a boil.

4 Add the lemon juice, hot-pepper sauce, seasoning, and bay leaf, then cover and simmer for 10 minutes. Coarsely chop half the shrimp, add to the soup, and simmer for 10 minutes longer.

5 Discard the bay leaf, stir in the milk and remaining shrimp and bring back to a boil. Simmer for 3–4 minutes. Adjust the seasoning and stir in the cream. Chill thoroughly.

6 Garnish with shrimp and chopped parsley, then serve.

FREEZING

Do not freeze this soup if the shrimp have been previously frozen.

16

CHAPTER TWO

Vegetable Soups

There is a huge variety of vegetable-based soups, so this chapter only covers a small selection. Vegetable soups can be rich and creamy, or light and delicate. The vegetables are often puréed to give a smooth consistency and thicken the soup, but you can also purée just half the mixture to give the soup more texture. Clear soups, such as French Onion Soup (see page 20) and Bortsch (see page 22), are often based on a richly flavored stock. For vegetarians, these soups should be made with a vegetable stock, but meat-eaters can use a good homemade chicken or meat stock, if preferred.

Try these recipes first following the recipes, then you can adapt them to make use of other vegetables – choose ingredients that are in season and soup-making can be extremely economical.

Opposite: *Cooking vegetables in a soup ensures little of their nutritional goodness is lost.*

FRENCH ONION SOUP

This classic French soup is packed with onions, which are cooked very slowly until they caramelize to give the soup its authentic, rich flavor. It is traditionally served with toasted cheese croutons.

STEP 1

STEP 2

STEP 3

STEP 5

SERVES 4

2 tbsp butter or margarine
2 tbsp oil
3 cups thinly sliced onions
1–2 garlic cloves, crushed
4¹/₃ cups strong Beef or Vegetable Stock (see
   pages 76–8)
2 bay leaves, preferably fresh
1 tbsp brown sugar
1 tbsp white-wine vinegar
good pinch ground allspice
8 thin slices French stick
¹/₂ cup grated Gruyère, Swiss, or Cheddar
   cheese
salt and pepper
chopped fresh parsley to garnish

1 Melt the butter or margarine and oil in a saucepan. Add the onions and garlic and fry very slowly for 10–15 minutes until soft.

2 Increase the heat a little and continue to fry, stirring frequently, until the onions turn a golden brown and become caramelized.

3 Add the stock and bring to a boil. Add the bay leaves, sugar, vinegar, seasoning, and allspice, cover the pan, and simmer for about 30 minutes.

4 Discard the bay leaves and adjust the seasoning. At this stage the soup may be cooled and chilled for up to 48 hours, or frozen for up to 6 weeks.

5 Toast 1 side of each slice of bread under a preheated broiler. Turn the slices over and sprinkle with the cheese. Put under the broiler until the cheese is bubbling.

6 Reheat the soup. Carefully ladle the soup into warmed soup bowls and float 2 slices of toasted bread on each portion. Sprinkle with chopped parsley. Allow the bread to soak up the soup a little and serve.

CARAMELIZING

Cooking the onions slowly over low heat is vital to the success of this soup. It allows the natural sugars in the onions to caramelize, which gives the soup its characteristic rich flavor and color.

STEP 1

STEP 2

STEP 5

STEP 6

BEET SOUPS

Here are two variations using the same vegetable: a creamy soup made with puréed, cooked beets; and a traditional Bortsch, a clear soup finished with a swirl of sour cream.

SERVES 4–6

BORTSCH:
1 lb raw beets, peeled and grated
2 carrots, chopped finely
1 large onion, chopped finely
1 garlic clove, crushed
1 Bouquet Garni (see page 78)
5 cups Chicken or Vegetable Stock (see pages 77–8)
2–3 tsp lemon juice
salt and pepper
$^2/_3$ cup sour cream to serve

CREAMED BEET SOUP:
$^1/_4$ cup butter or margarine
2 large onions, chopped finely
1–2 carrots, chopped
2 celery stalks, chopped
4 cups cooked diced beetroot
1–2 tbsp lemon juice
$3^1/_2$ cups Chicken, Beef or Vegetable Stock (see pages 76–8)
$1^1/_4$ cups milk
salt and pepper
grated cooked beets or 6 tbsp sour or heavy cream, lightly whipped, to serve

1 To make bortsch, place the beets, carrots, onion, garlic, bouquet garni, stock, lemon juice, and seasoning in a saucepan. Bring to a boil, then cover and simmer for 45 minutes.

2 Press the soup through a fine strainer or a strainer lined with cheesecloth, then pour it into a clean pan. Adjust the seasoning and add extra lemon juice if necessary.

3 Bring to a boil, then simmer for 1–2 minutes. Serve with a spoonful of sour cream swirled through.

4 To make creamed beet soup, melt the butter or margarine in a saucepan and fry the onions, carrots, and celery until just beginning to color.

5 Add the beets, 1 tablespoon of the lemon juice, the stock, and seasoning and bring to a boil. Cover and simmer for 30 minutes until tender.

6 Cool slightly, then press it through a strainer or blend it in a food processor or blender. Pour into a clean pan. Add the milk and bring to a boil. Adjust the seasoning, add extra lemon juice if necessary and serve topped with grated beet or sour or heavy cream.

STEP 1

STEP 4

STEP 4

STEP 5

CREAMED PARSNIP & TARRAGON SOUP

The creamy texture and subtle flavouring of this soup will make it a favorite with everyone, for everyday meals or special occasions.

SERVES 4–6

1 carrot
1 lb parsnips
3 tbsp butter or margarine
1 large onion, chopped
1 garlic clove, crushed (optional)
3½ cups Chicken or Vegetable Stock (see pages 77–8)
2 tbsp lemon juice
2–3 sprigs fresh tarragon or 2 tsp dried tarragon
1¼ cups milk
²⁄₃ cup natural fromage frais or light cream
2 tsp chopped fresh tarragon
salt and pepper
Fried Croutons (see page 79) to serve

1 Peel the carrot and slice. Peel the parsnips and cut into chunks.

2 Melt the butter or margarine in a large saucepan and fry the onion and garlic, if using, until soft but not colored.

3 Add the parsnips and carrot and continue to fry for a few minutes, tossing the vegetables and stirring frequently.

4 Add the stock and bring to a boil; add the seasoning, lemon juice, and tarragon, then cover and simmer for about 30 minutes until the vegetables are very tender.

5 Discard the fresh tarragon sprigs, if using, and cool the soup a little, then press it through a strainer or blend in a food processor or blender until smooth.

6 Pour into a clean saucepan and add the milk. Bring slowly to a boil. Beat the fromage frais, if using, until smooth and add this or the cream to the soup and reheat again slowly but do not let boil. Adjust the seasoning and stir in half the chopped tarragon. Serve the soup with the fried croutons and the remaining tarragon sprinkled on top.

FREEZING

This soup can be frozen for up to 3 months. Add the fromage frais or cream when reheating.

CREAMED CARROT & CUMIN SOUP

*Carrot soups are very popular and are always an attractive color.
Flavorings can vary widely but here cumin, tomato, potato, and celery
give the soup both richness and depth of flavor.*

STEP 2

SERVES 4–6

3 tbsp butter or margarine
1 large onion, chopped
1–2 garlic cloves, crushed
2¹/₂ cups sliced carrots
3¹/₂ cups Chicken or Vegetable Stock (see
  pages 77–8)
³/₄ tsp ground cumin
2 celery stalks, sliced thinly
1 cup diced potato
2 tsp tomato paste
2 tsp lemon juice
2 fresh or dried bay leaves
about 1¹/₄ cups milk
salt and pepper
celery leaves to garnish

1 Melt the butter or margarine in a
large saucepan. Add the onion and
garlic and fry very gently until the onion
begins to soften.

2 Add the carrots and continue to fry
gently for 5 minutes longer,
stirring frequently and taking care they
do not brown.

3 Add the stock, cumin, seasoning,
celery, potato, tomato paste, lemon
juice, and bay leaves, then bring to a boil.
Cover and simmer for about 30 minutes

until all the vegetables are very tender.

4 Discard the bay leaves, and cool
the soup a little, then press it
through a strainer or blend it in a food
processor or blender until smooth.

5 Pour the soup into a clean pan, add
the milk, and bring slowly to a boil.
Taste and adjust the seasoning.

6 Garnish each serving with a small
celery leaf and serve.

STEP 3

STEP 4

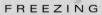

FREEZING

This soup can be frozen for up to 3
months. Add the milk when reheating.

STEP 5

STEP 1

STEP 2

STEP 4

STEP 6

CREAM OF JERUSALEM ARTICHOKE SOUP

A creamy soup with a garnish of grated carrots for extra crunch. This is considered by many to be the best of all vegetable soups.

SERVES 4–6

5¹/₂ cups Chicken or Vegetable Stock (see pages 77–8)
1¹/₂ lb Jerusalem artichokes
1 lemon, sliced thickly
¹/₄ cup butter or margarine
2 onions, chopped
1 garlic clove, crushed
2 bay leaves, preferably fresh
¹/₄ tsp ground mace or grated nutmeg
1 tbsp lemon juice
²/₃ cup light cream or natural fromage frais
salt and pepper

TO GARNISH:
coarsely grated carrot
chopped fresh parsley or cilantro

1 Make the stock, if necessary (see pages 77–8).

2 Peel and slice the artichokes. Put them into a bowl of water with the lemon slices.

3 Melt the butter or margarine in a large saucepan. Add the onions and garlic and fry slowly for 3–4 minutes until soft but not colored.

4 Drain the artichokes and add to the pan. Mix well and cook slowly for 2–3 minutes without letting them color.

5 Add the stock, seasoning, bay leaves, mace or nutmeg, and lemon juice, then bring slowly to a boil. Cover and simmer for about 30 minutes until the vegetables are very tender.

6 Remove the bay leaves and cool slightly, then press the soup through a strainer or blend in a food processor or blender until smooth. If liked, a little of the soup may be only partially puréed and added to the rest of the puréed soup, to give extra texture.

7 Pour into a clean pan and bring to a boil. Adjust the seasoning and stir in the cream or fromage frais. Reheat gently without boiling. Garnish with grated carrot and chopped parsley or cilantro and serve.

FREEZING

This soup can be frozen for up to 3 months. Add the cream or fromage frais when reheating.

PUMPKIN SOUP

This is a fall classic that has now become popular worldwide. With its subtle flavor and attractive orange color, it will soon become a firm favorite with you, too. When pumpkin is out of season, use butternut squash in its place.

STEP 1

STEP 3

STEP 5

STEP 6

SERVES 4–6

about 2 lb pumpkin
3 tbsp butter or margarine
1 onion, sliced thinly
1 garlic clove, crushed
3¹/₂ cups Chicken or Vegetable Stock (see
    pages 77–8)
¹/₂ tsp ground ginger
1 tbsp lemon juice
3–4 thinly pared strips orange rind
    (optional)
1–2 fresh or dried bay leaves or 1 Bouquet
    Garni (see page 78)
1¹/₄ cups milk
salt and pepper

TO GARNISH:
4–6 tablespoons light or heavy cream, plain
    yogurt or fromage frais
snipped chives

1 Peel the pumpkin, remove the seeds, and cut the flesh into 1-in. cubes.

2 Melt the butter or margarine in a large saucepan. Add the onion and garlic and fry slowly until soft but not colored.

3 Add the pumpkin and stir-fry with the onion for a few minutes.

4 Add the stock and bring to a boil. Add the seasoning, ginger, lemon juice, strips of orange rind, if using, and bay leaves or bouquet garni, then cover and simmer for about 20 minutes until the pumpkin is very tender.

5 Discard the orange rind, if using, and the bay leaves or bouquet garni. Cool the soup a little and then press it through a strainer or blend in a food processor or blender until smooth. Pour it into a clean saucepan.

6 Add the milk and reheat gently. Adjust the seasoning. Garnish with a swirl of cream, plain yogurt, or fromage frais and snipped chives and serve.

PUMPKINS

Pumpkins are usually sold whole but if they are very large you may be able to buy just a half or a quarter.

STEP 2

STEP 3

STEP 6

STEP 7

GARDENER'S BROTH

This thick, hearty soup uses a variety of green vegetables with a flavoring of ground coriander. A finishing touch of thinly sliced leeks adds texture.

SERVES 4–6

3 tbsp butter or margarine
1 onion, chopped
1–2 garlic cloves, crushed
1 large leek
8 oz brussels sprouts
4 oz green or runner beans
5 cups Vegetable or Chicken Stock (see pages 77–8)
³/₄ cup frozen peas
1 tbsp lemon juice
¹/₂ tsp ground coriander
4 tbsp heavy cream
salt and pepper

MELBA TOAST:
4–6 slices white bread

1 Melt the butter or margarine in a saucepan. Add the onion and garlic and fry very slowly, stirring occasionally, until they begin to soften but not color.

2 Slice the white part of the leek very thinly and reserve; slice the remaining leeks. Slice the brussels sprouts and thinly slice the beans.

3 Add the green part of the leeks, the brussels sprouts, and the beans to the saucepan. Add the stock and bring to a boil, then simmer for 10 minutes.

4 Add the frozen peas, seasoning, lemon juice, and coriander and continue to simmer for 10–15 minutes until the vegetables are tender.

5 Cool the soup a little, then press it through a strainer or blend in a food processor or blender until smooth. Pour it into a clean pan.

6 Add the reserved leek slices to the soup and bring back to a boil, then simmer for about 5 minutes until the leeks are tender. Adjust the seasoning, stir in the cream, and reheat gently.

7 Make the Melba toast. Toast the bread on both sides under a preheated broiler. Cut horizontally through the slices, then toast the uncooked sides until they curl up. Serve immediately with the soup.

FREEZING

This soup can be frozen for up to 2 months. Add the cream when reheating.

CHAPTER THREE

Fish Soups

Fish soups are particularly popular and can be made with a huge variety of fish and shellfish. Many are so full of fish that they need a fork, as well as a spoon, to eat them. They often include shellfish, such as mussels and shrimp, so a bowl for the discarded "debris" is often required on the table, plus a finger bowl and napkin for cleaning up afterwards.

As with most soups, the basis of a good fish soup is a good stock. It may seem a bit of trouble to make Fish Stock (see page 77), but it is often possible to buy fish heads and trimmings which are ideal for homemade stock, and it is much quicker to make than other stocks — it only needs 30 minutes of simmering. But if you don't have the time, some supermarkets sell fresh fish stock and there are now good fish stock cubes available, both of which can be used as alternatives. Chicken or vegetable stock can also be used.

It is best to make soups from fresh fish. Although specialist fish merchants are becoming more rare, many larger supermarkets now have impressive wet-fish counters. Frozen fish can be used if necessary, but if you want to freeze the soup, make sure the fish has been well cooked.

Opposite: *Shellfish such as mussels and shrimp do not keep well and should be prepared and cooked as soon as possible after buying.*

STEP 1

STEP 3

STEP 4

STEP 6

BOUILLABAISSE

This classic French soup is traditionally made from at least eight varieties of fish and shellfish. Many of those, unfortunately, are only available from the Mediterranean, but you should be able to get a good enough selection from your fish merchant or supermarket.

SERVES 4–6

1½–2 lb mixed fish and shellfish, such as whiting, mackerel, red or gray mullet, cod, eel, sea bass, crab, shrimp, lobster, scampi, and mussels
2 large onions, sliced thinly or chopped
2 celery stalks, sliced very thinly
1 carrot, chopped finely
2–3 garlic cloves, crushed
4 tbsp olive oil
14-oz can crushed tomatoes with mixed herbs or 1½ cups skinned and chopped fresh tomatoes,
1 fresh or dried bay leaf
¼ tsp ground coriander
few sprigs fresh mixed herbs, including parsley
1 tsp grated lemon rind
1–2 tbsp lemon juice
about 1¼ cups water
pinch saffron threads or ground turmeric
salt and pepper
chopped mixed herbs to garnish

1 Clean the fish, removing any skin and visible bones, and cut into 2 x 1-in. pieces. Remove shellfish from their shells.

2 Slowly fry the onions, celery, carrot, and garlic in the oil in a large saucepan for about 5 minutes until soft but not colored.

3 Stir in the tomatoes, bay leaf, coriander, herbs, seasoning, and lemon rind and juice.

4 Arrange all the fish and shellfish in the pan over the vegetables.

5 Put the measured water in another saucepan, add the saffron or turmeric and bring to a boil. Pour into the saucepan of fish, adding enough to just cover the fish.

6 Bring to a boil, then cover and simmer for about 20 minutes until the fish is tender but not broken up.

7 Discard the bay leaf and herbs, then ladle the soup into bowls, sprinkle with the chopped mixed herbs, and serve. Both a soup spoon and fork are needed to eat this soup.

MOULES MARINIERE

A true French soup of mussels cooked in white wine with onions, garlic, herbs, and cream. It can be served as an appetizer or a main dish, with plenty of warm crusty bread.

STEP 1

STEP 3

STEP 4

STEP 5

SERVES 4

about 6 pints fresh mussels
¹/₄ cup butter
1 large onion, chopped very finely
2–3 garlic cloves, crushed
1¹/₂ cups dry white wine
²/₃ cup water
2 tbsp lemon juice
good pinch finely grated lemon rind
1 Bouquet Garni (see page 78)
1 tbsp all-purpose flour
4 tbsp light or heavy cream
2–3 tbsp chopped fresh parsley
salt and pepper
warm crusty bread to serve

1 Scrub the mussels in several changes of cold water to remove all mud, sand, and barnacles. Pull off all the "beards". All the mussels must be tightly closed; if they don't close when given a sharp tap, they must be discarded.

2 Melt half the butter in a large saucepan. Add the onion and garlic and fry slowly until soft but not colored.

3 Add the wine, water, lemon juice and rind, bouquet garni, and plenty of seasoning and bring to a boil. Cover and simmer for 4–5 minutes.

4 Add the mussels to the pan, cover tightly, and simmer for 5 minutes, shaking the pan frequently, until all the mussels have opened. Discard any mussels which have not opened and remove the bouquet garni.

5 Remove the empty half shell from each mussel. Blend the remaining butter with the flour and whisk into the soup, a little at a time. Simmer for 2–3 minutes until slightly thickened.

6 Add the cream and half the parsley to the soup and reheat slowly. Adjust the seasoning. Ladle the mussels and soup into warmed, large soup bowls, sprinkle with the remaining parsley and serve with plenty of warm crusty bread.

MUSSELS

Before cooking mussels it is important to discard any that are not closed, beause they are dead. Similarly, be sure to discard any which do not open during cooking.

PARTAN BREE

This traditional Scottish soup is thickened with a purée of rice and crabmeat cooked in milk. Extra crabmeat is added with fresh herbs and a little sour cream, if liked, at the end of cooking.

STEP 1

SERVES 4–6

1 medium-size boiled crab
scant ¹/₂ cup long-grain rice
2¹/₂ cups milk
2¹/₂ cups Fish Stock (see page 77)
1 tbsp anchovy paste
2 tsp lime or lemon juice
1 tbsp chopped fresh parsley or 1 tsp chopped
    fresh thyme
3–4 tbsp sour cream (optional)
salt and pepper
snipped fresh chives to garnish

1 Remove and reserve all the brown and white meat from the crab, then crack the claws and remove and chop that meat; reserve the claw meat.

2 Put the rice and milk into a saucepan and bring slowly to a boil. Cover and simmer gently for about 20 minutes until the rice is very tender.

3 Add the reserved white and brown crabmeats and seasoning, then simmer for 5 minutes longer.

4 Cool the mixture a little, then press it through a strainer, or blend in a food processor or blender until smooth.

5 Pour the soup into a clean saucepan and add the fish stock and the reserved claw meat. Bring slowly to a boil, then add the anchovy paste and lime or lemon juice and adjust the seasoning.

6 Simmer for 2–3 minutes longer. Stir in the parsley or thyme and then swirl sour cream, if using, through each serving. Garnish with snipped chives.

STEP 3

CRAB

Cooked crabs are available from fish merchants and larger supermarkets. They are also available frozen from some stores. If you are unable to buy a whole crab, use about 6 oz frozen crabmeat, which must be thoroughly thawed before use; or a 6-oz can of crabmeat, which just needs thorough draining and flaking before use.

STEP 5

STEP 6

SHRIMP GUMBO

*This soup is thick with onions, red bell peppers, rice, shrimp, and okra,
which both adds flavor and acts as a thickening agent.*

STEP 1

STEP 2

STEP 3

STEP 4

SERVES 4–6

1 large onion, chopped finely
2 slices lean bacon, chopped finely (optional)
1–2 garlic cloves, crushed
2 tbsp olive oil
1 large or 2 small red bell peppers, chopped
    finely
3¹/₂ cups Fish or Vegetable Stock (see pages
    77–8)
1 fresh or dried bay leaf
1 blade mace
good pinch ground allspice
3 tbsp long-grain rice
1 tbsp white-wine vinegar
1¹/₂–1³/₄ cups trimmed and very thinly
    sliced okra
¹/₂–²/₃ cup cooked, peeled shrimp
1 tbsp anchovy paste
2 tsp tomato paste
1–2 tbsp chopped fresh parsley
salt and pepper
Cheese & Anchovy Twists (see page 79) to
    serve

TO GARNISH:
whole shrimp
fresh parsley sprigs

1 Slowly fry the onion, bacon, if using, and garlic in the oil in a large saucepan for 4–5 minutes until soft, but only lightly colored. Add the bell peppers to the pan and continue to fry gently for a couple of minutes.

2 Add the stock, bay leaf, mace, allspice, rice, vinegar, and seasoning and bring to a boil. Cover and simmer for about 20 minutes, giving an occasional stir, until the rice is just tender.

3 Add the okra, shrimp, anchovy paste, and tomato paste, then cover and simmer gently for about 15 minutes until the okra is tender and the mixture slightly thickened.

4 Meanwhile, make the cheese and anchovy twists (see page 79).

5 Discard the bay leaf and mace from the soup and adjust the seasoning. Stir in the parsley and serve each portion garnished with a whole shrimp and parsley sprigs. Serve with warm cheese and anchovy twists.

STEP 1

STEP 3

STEP 5

STEP 6

SMOKY HADDOCK SOUP

Smoked haddock gives this soup a good, rich flavor, while mashed potatoes and cream thicken and enrich the stock.

SERVES 4–6

8 oz smoked haddock fillet
1 onion, chopped finely
1 garlic clove, crushed
2¹/₂ cups water
2¹/₂ cups milk
1–1¹/₂ cups hot mashed potatoes
2 tbsp butter
about 1 tbsp lemon juice
6 tbsp heavy cream, sour cream or plain
    yogurt
4 tbsp chopped fresh parsley
salt and pepper

1 Put the fish, onion, garlic, and water into a saucepan. Bring to a boil, then cover the pan and simmer for 15–20 minutes until the fish is tender.

2 Remove the fish from the pan; strip off the skin and remove all the bones. Flake the flesh finely.

3 Return the skin and bones to the cooking liquid and simmer for 10 minutes. Strain and pour the liquid into a clean pan.

4 Add the milk, flaked fish, and seasoning to the pan. Bring to a boil, then lower the heat and simmer for about 3 minutes.

5 Gradually whisk in sufficient mashed potato to give a fairly thick soup, then stir in the butter and sharpen to taste with lemon juice.

6 Add the cream, sour cream, or plain yogurt and 3 tablespoons of the chopped parsley. Reheat slowly and adjust the seasoning. Sprinkle with the remaining parsley and serve.

SMOKED HADDOCK

Undyed smoked haddock can be used in place of the bright yellow fish; it will give a paler color but just as much flavor. Alternatively, use smoked cod or smoked whiting.

STEP 1

STEP 3

STEP 5

STEP 6

SALMON BISQUE

A filling soup which is ideal for all types of occasion, from an elegant dinner to a picnic. This can be made from salmon heads or pieces and, for a touch of luxury, garnished with smoked salmon.

SERVES 4–6

1–2 salmon heads (depending on size), or a
   tail piece of salmon weighing about 1 lb
3½ cups water
1 fresh or dried bay leaf
1 lemon, sliced
a few black peppercorns
2 tbsp butter or margarine
2 tbsp finely chopped onion or scallions
¼ cup all-purpose flour
⅔ cup dry white wine or Fish Stock (see
   page 77)
⅔ cup light cream
1 tbsp chopped fresh fennel or dill
2–3 tsp lemon or lime juice
salt and pepper

TO GARNISH:
1–1½ oz smoked salmon pieces, chopped
   (optional)
fresh fennel or dill sprigs

1 Put the salmon, water, bay leaf, lemon, and peppercorns into a saucepan. Bring to a boil and remove any scum from the surface, then cover the pan and simmer for 20 minutes.

2 Remove from the heat, strain the stock and reserve 2½ cups.

3 Remove and discard all the skin and bones from the salmon and flake the flesh, removing all the pieces from the head, if using.

4 Melt the butter or margarine in a saucepan and fry the onion or scallions slowly for about 5 minutes until soft. Stir in the flour and cook for 1 minute, then gradually stir in the reserved stock and wine or fish stock. Bring to a boil, stirring.

5 Add the salmon and season well, then simmer for about 5 minutes.

6 Add the cream and the chopped fennel or dill and reheat, but do not boil. Sharpen to taste with lemon or lime juice and adjust the seasoning. Serve hot or chilled, garnished with smoked salmon, if using, and sprigs of fennel or dill.

CHAPTER FOUR

Chowders

A chowder is a thick and chunky soup, full of chopped vegetables, meat, fish, shellfish, pasta or rice, substantial enough to suit meat-eaters and vegetarians alike. Hearty and filling, it is usually served as a snack or a meal in itself, rather than as a first course.

Again it is important to use a well-flavored stock as the base for a chowder. The thickening agent may be a roux, a beurre manié (see page 79), or a blend of egg yolks and cream (see page 79). Rice, barley, potatoes, or a purée of some of the soup also thicken chowders.

These soups are an excellent way to use up leftovers, whether meat, fish or vegetables. Vegetables are used in many forms: they may be finely chopped or diced, thinly sliced, cut into thin strips, or coarsely grated. A food processor is a useful piece of equipment for preparing the vegetables in the minimum of time. If raw meat is added, it should be minced or ground and added at the start of cooking. Raw poultry and fish need only be chopped, but again added early in the cooking process. Cooked meats, poultry, and fish can be added part way through cooking but also need to be minced or ground.

Opposite: *Chunky vegetables are an important part of a chowder. Make sure you cut them into even-size pieces so they cook evenly.*

STEP 1

STEP 2

STEP 3

STEP 5

HOLLANDAISE-OAT CHOWDER

An unusual soup made with chunky vegetables and steel-cut oats and given a little bite by adding vinegar and mayonnaise. Oatcakes are the ideal accompaniment.

SERVES 4–6

^{1}/$_4$ cup butter or margarine
2 large onions, chopped finely or sliced very
    thinly
1 garlic clove, crushed
1 turnip
3 carrots
3 celery stalks and/or 6 oz celery root
1 leek
^{1}/$_2$ cup steel-cut oats
4^1/$_2$ cups stock
^{2}/$_3$ cup milk
about 2 tbsp white-wine vinegar
1 egg yolk
^{2}/$_3$ cup light cream
2 tbsp mayonnaise
salt and pepper
chopped fresh mixed herbs to garnish
oatcakes to serve

1 Melt the butter or margarine in a saucepan and lightly fry the onions and garlic for about 10 minutes until very soft but not colored.

2 Finely chop the turnip, carrots, and celery and/or celery root. Thinly slice the leek.

3 Add the vegetables to the pan and continue to fry, stirring from time to time, for about 5 minutes. Add the oats and cook for 1 minute longer. Add the stock and then the milk and bring to a boil.

4 Season well, add 2 tablespoons of vinegar, cover, and simmer for about 30 minutes until the vegetables are very tender.

5 Mix the egg yolk with the cream, add a little of the soup to the cream, and then whisk it all back into the soup, followed by the mayonnaise.

6 Bring slowly back just to a boil, adjust the seasoning and add extra vinegar, if necessary, to sharpen the taste. Sprinkle with plenty of chopped mixed herbs and serve with oatcakes.

VARIATION

This soup can be varied by adding 3/4–1 cup crumbled blue cheese in place of the cream and egg yolk, and by adding an extra 2/3 cup milk or stock in place of the cream.

STEP 2

STEP 3

STEP 4

STEP 5

CURRIED COD CHOWDER

Chunks of white fish cooked with root vegetables and rice and flavoured with tomatoes and curry powder.

SERVES 4–6

2 tbsp butter or margarine
1 tbsp olive oil
1 onion, chopped finely
2 celery sticks, chopped finely
1 garlic clove, crushed
1½ tsp medium hot curry powder
3 cups Fish or Vegetable Stock (see pages 77–8)
1 fresh or dried bay leaf
12 oz haddock or cod fillet, skinned and chopped coarsely
14-oz can crushed tomatoes
1 tbsp tomato paste
¼ cup long-grain rice
1 carrot, grated coarsely
2 tsp lemon juice
4 tbsp light or heavy cream or natural fromage frais
2 tsp chopped fresh mixed herbs
salt and pepper
crusty bread to serve

1 Melt the butter or margarine with the oil in a saucepan, add the onion, celery, and garlic and fry until soft but not coloured.

2 Stir in the curry powder, cook for 1 minute and then add the stock, bay leaf, and seasoning. Bring to a boil.

3 Add the fish, cover and simmer for about 10 minutes until the flesh flakes easily.

4 Break up the fish, then add the tomatoes, tomato paste, rice, carrot, and lemon juice. Bring back to a boil, then cover and simmer for 20 minutes until the rice is tender.

5 Stir in the cream or fromage frais and the herbs and adjust the seasoning. Reheat and serve with plenty of crusty bread.

VARIATION

Shrimp, smoked fish or salmon, or a mixture of fish may also be used for this chowder.

52

COCK-A-LEEKIE SOUP

A traditional Scottish soup in which a whole chicken is cooked with the vegetables to add extra flavor to the stock. Add some of the cooked chicken to the soup and reserve the remainder for another meal.

STEP 1

SERVES 4–6

2–3 lb dressed chicken, plus giblets, if available
about 1 quart Chicken Stock (see page 77)
1 onion, chopped very finely
4 leeks, sliced thinly
good pinch ground allspice or ground coriander
1 Bouquet Garni (see page 78)
12 no-need-to-soak prunes, halved and pitted
salt and pepper
warm crusty bread to serve

1 Put the chicken, giblets, if using, stock, and onion in a large saucepan.

2 Bring to a boil and remove any foam from the surface.

3 Add the leeks, seasoning, allspice or coriander, and bouquet garni to the pan, cover, and simmer for about 1½ hours until the chicken is falling off the bones.

4 Remove the chicken from the pan and skim any fat from the surface of the soup.

5 Chop some of the chicken flesh and return to the pan. Add the prunes and bring back to a boil, then simmer, uncovered, for about 20 minutes.

6 Discard the bouquet garni, adjust the seasoning, and serve.

STEP 3

STEP 4

VARIATION

You can replace the chicken stock with 3 chicken stock cubes dissolved in the same amount of water, if you prefer.

STEP 5

SAGE & ONION CHOWDER

A thick, creamy onion soup full of chopped bacon, potatoes, and corn kernels with plenty of fragrant fresh sage.

STEP 1

STEP 2

STEP 3

STEP 4

SERVES 4–6

1/4 cup butter or margarine
4 onions, sliced very thinly or chopped
1–2 garlic cloves, crushed
4 slices lean bacon, chopped
2 tbsp all-purpose flour
3 1/2 cups Chicken or Vegetable Stock (see
    pages 77–8)
3 cups very finely diced potatoes
2/3 cup milk
7-oz can whole-kernel corn, well drained
1 tbsp chopped fresh sage or 1 1/2 tsp dried
    sage
2 tbsp white-wine vinegar
salt and pepper
fresh sage sprigs to garnish
Cheese Biscuits (see pages 77–8), warmed,
    to serve

1 Melt the butter or margarine in a large saucepan and fry the onions and garlic very slowly for about 10 minutes until soft but not colored.

2 Add the bacon and continue to fry for a few minutes, allowing the onions to color a little. Stir in the flour and cook for 1 minute longer.

3 Add the stock and bring to a boil, then add the potatoes and seasoning and simmer for 20 minutes.

4 Add the milk and corn kernels and bring back to a boil, then add the sage and vinegar and simmer for 10–15 minutes longer until the potatoes are very tender but not broken up.

5 Adjust the seasoning, garnish with sprigs of sage, and serve with warmed cheese biscuits.

VARIATION

Frozen corn kernels can be used instead of the canned variety. Add to the soup in step 4 — there's no need to thaw them first.

STEP 1

STEP 3

STEP 4

STEP 5

RED BEAN CHOWDER

A real hearty chowder full of mixed chopped vegetables and ground beef and spiced with chili powder. This recipe uses dried beans but if you're short of time, use canned beans instead.

SERVES 4–6

1 cup dried red kidney beans, soaked
  overnight and drained or 14-oz can red
  kidney beans, drained
3¹/₂ cups water if using dried beans
3 tbsp butter or margarine
1 large onion, chopped very finely
1 large carrot, chopped finely
1–2 celery stalks, chopped finely
1 small turnip, chopped finely
2 garlic cloves, crushed
6 oz extra lean finely ground beef
2 tbsp all-purpose flour
1–2 tsp chili powder
3¹/₂ cups Beef Stock (see page 77)
2 tsp tomato paste
4 tomatoes, skinned and chopped finely
1 tsp chopped fresh oregano or ¹/₂ tsp dried
  oregano
salt and pepper
warm crusty bread to serve

1 If using dried kidney beans, put them in a saucepan with the water, bring to a boil, and boil hard for 10–15 minutes. Reduce the heat and simmer for 1–1¹/₂ hours until tender, then drain.

2 Melt the butter or margarine in a saucepan and fry the onion, carrot, celery, turnip, and garlic very slowly for

about 10 minutes until soft.

3 Add the beef and cook slowly, stirring frequently, for 10 minutes until cooked and lightly browned.

4 Stir in the flour and chili powder and cook for 2 minutes. Gradually stir in the stock and tomato paste and bring to a boil, stirring.

5 Season the chowder, cover the pan, and simmer for 30 minutes. Stir in the tomatoes, oregano, and beans.

6 Return to a boil, then simmer for 5 minutes. If the soup seems very thick, add a little more boiling water or stock. Adjust the seasoning and serve with warm crusty bread.

DRIED RED KIDNEY BEANS

If using dried red kidney beans it is essential that they are boiled hard for at least 10 minutes to kill any toxins; they are then simmered until tender.

CHAPTER FIVE

Meat & Poultry Soups

Meat soups and broths are all based on some type of meat stock, be it made from beef bones, a poultry carcass, game, or a ham bone, and it is important that the stock is strongly flavored. It is essential not to add too much extra meat to the soup, however, as the texture will be spoiled and the soup may be too thick and heavy.

Onions, garlic, and a good bouquet garni or bay leaves are very important in these soups, and where herbs are called for, fresh ones give a much better flavor. Because dried herbs have a more intense flavor, if you do use them, however, you should use roughly half the quantity of fresh herbs. Fresh herbs also make attractive garnishes: float some leaves or sprigs on top of the soup just before serving, or sprinkle the soup with chopped herbs to add a splash of freshness and color.

Opposite: Meat soups are an economical choice as the long, slow cooking means you can use cheaper cuts of meat.

STEP 1

STEP 3

STEP 5

STEP 5

CHICKEN & CHESTNUT SOUP

A rich soup based on a good stock with pieces of chicken and chopped chestnuts for an interesting flavor and texture.

SERVES 4–6

2 onions
1 raw or cooked chicken carcass, chopped, plus trimmings
chicken giblets, if available
6¼ cups water
1 Bouquet Garni (see page 78)
½ cup fresh chestnuts, pierced and roasted for about 5 minutes, or boiled for 30–40 minutes, drained, or 1 cup canned peeled chestnuts
3 tbsp butter or margarine
⅓ cup all-purpose flour
⅔ cup milk
½ tsp ground coriander
1½ cups coarsely grated carrots
1 tbsp chopped fresh parsley (optional)
salt and pepper

1 Cut 1 of the onions into quarters. Put the chicken carcass, giblets, if available, water, the quartered onion, and bouquet garni into a saucepan. Bring to a boil, then cover and simmer for about 1 hour, stirring occasionally.

2 Strain the stock and reserve 1 quart.

3 Remove ½–¾ cup of chicken trimmings from the carcass and chop finely. If using fresh chestnuts, peel them; if using canned chestnuts, drain them well. Finely chop the chestnuts. Chop the remaining onion.

4 Melt the butter or margarine in a saucepan and fry the onion gently until soft. Stir in the flour and cook for 1 minute or so.

5 Gradually stir in the reserved stock and bring to a boil, stirring. Lower the heat and simmer for 2 minutes, then add the milk, seasoning, coriander, chopped chicken, carrots, and chestnuts.

6 Bring back to a boil, then simmer for 10 minutes. Stir in the parsley, if using. Adjust the seasoning and serve.

CHICKEN CARCASS

For this soup, use a carcass that still has a certain amount of meat left on the bones. Otherwise use 1 or 2 chicken portions and 4–6 chicken stock cubes.

CREAMED PHEASANT SOUP

This is a rich, creamy soup flavored with onion, garlic, and mushrooms, and is ideal for using up a leftover pheasant carcass. If you prefer, you can use a whole bird.

STEP 1

STEP 4

STEP 5

STEP 6

SERVES 4–6

1 raw or cooked pheasant carcass or 1 small
   dressed pheasant
1 onion, studded with 6 cloves
6¼ cups water
¼ cup butter or margarine
1 onion, chopped finely
⅓ cup all-purpose flour
½ tsp celery salt
¼ tsp ground coriander
2 tbsp long-grain rice
2 cups finely chopped mushrooms
⅔ cup light or heavy cream
2 tbsp chopped fresh parsley
salt and pepper
Fried Croutons (see page 79) to serve

1 Put the pheasant carcass or the whole bird, the clove-studded onion, and the water into a saucepan. Bring to a boil, then cover and simmer for about 1½ hours. Drain off and reserve 5½ cups of the stock. Remove about ½ cup of meat from the carcass or from the leg or wing of the whole bird; chop it finely.

2 Melt the butter or margarine in a saucepan and fry the chopped onion slowly for about 3 minutes until soft but not colored.

3 Stir in the flour and cook for 1 minute or so, then gradually stir in the reserved stock and bring to a boil.

4 Add the seasoning, celery salt, coriander, rice, and mushrooms, cover, and simmer for about 20 minutes, stirring occasionally.

5 Add the reserved pheasant meat and the cream, adjust the seasoning, and bring back just to a boil.

6 Just before serving, stir in the parsley or, if preferred, stir in half the parsley and use the remainder to sprinkle over each serving. Serve with fried croutons.

FREEZING

This soup can be frozen for up to 2 months. Add the cream and parsley when reheating.

STEP 1

STEP 2

STEP 4

STEP 4

CONSOMME

A traditional clear soup made from beef bones and lean ground beef. Thin strips of vegetables provide a colorful garnish.

SERVES 4–6

5½ cups strong Beef Stock (see page 77)
8 oz extra lean ground beef
2 tomatoes, skinned, deseeded and chopped
2 large carrots, chopped
1 large onion, chopped
2 celery sticks, chopped
1 turnip, chopped (optional)
1 Bouquet Garni (see page 78)
2–3 egg whites
shells of 2–4 eggs, crushed
1–2 tbsp dry sherry (optional)
salt and pepper
Melba Toast (see page 32) to serve

TO GARNISH:
julienne strips of raw carrot, turnip, celery
   or celery root, or a one-egg omelet, cut
   into julienne strips

1 Make the stock, if necessary (see page 76). Put the stock and ground beef in a saucepan and leave to stand for 1 hour.

2 Add the tomatoes, carrots, onion, celery, turnip, if using, bouquet garni, 2 of the egg whites, the crushed shells of 2 of the eggs, and plenty of seasoning. Bring almost to boiling point, whisking all the time with a flat whisk.

3 Cover and simmer for 1 hour, taking care not to allow the layer of froth on top of the soup to break.

4 Pour through a jelly bag or scalded fine cloth, keeping the froth back until the last, then pour again through the egg shells in the cloth into a clean pan. The resulting liquid should be clear.

5 If the soup is not quite clear, return it to the pan with another egg white and the crushed shells of 2 more eggs. Repeat the whisking process as before and boil for 10 minutes; strain again.

6 Add the sherry to the soup and reheat without boiling.

7 Place the garnish in the base of warmed soup bowls and carefully pour in the soup. Serve with Melba toast.

STEP 1

STEP 3

STEP 4

STEP 5

SCOTCH BROTH

This old-fashioned and traditional soup from Scotland was originally made with a sheep's head but stewing lamb is now used. It is cooked slowly with a selection of root vegetables, pearl barley, and parsley. The lamb may be quite fatty so be sure to skim the surface well.

SERVES 6

1½–2 lb stewing lamb on the bone
2¼ quarts water
2 fresh or dried bay leaves
1¼ cups finely chopped carrots
1 turnip, chopped
2 onions, chopped finely
2 leeks, sliced very thinly
¾–1½ cups finely diced potatoes
¼ cup pearl barley
salt and pepper
3 tbsp chopped fresh parsley to garnish

1 Trim the meat, removing any excess fat. Put in a large saucepan with the water and bring to a boil.

2 Remove any foam from the surface, then add the bay leaves and plenty of seasoning. Cover and simmer for 1½ hours.

3 Add all the vegetables and the barley, stir and bring back to a gentle simmer. Cover the pan and simmer for 1 hour until the barley and vegetables are very soft.

4 Cool slightly, then skim the fat from the surface. Remove the last of the fat by placing paper towels on the surface to absorb the fat.

5 Adjust the seasoning. Remove the lamb, strip the meat from the bones, and return it to the soup. Alternatively, the pieces of meat can be served still on the bone: put a piece of meat in each serving bowl and ladle the soup over (a fork will then be required to eat the soup).

6 Sprinkle the parsley over each portion and serve.

REMOVING THE FAT

If time allows, leave the soup to cool after step 3. It will then be easy to lift the solidified fat from the surface.

LENTIL & HAM SOUP

This is a good, hearty soup, ideal for a cold winter's day. It is based on a stock made from a ham knuckle, with plenty of vegetables and red lentils to thicken it and add flavor.

STEP 2

STEP 3

STEP 4

SERVES 4–6

1¼ cups red lentils
6¼ cups stock or water
2 onions, chopped
1 garlic clove, crushed
2 large carrots, chopped
1 ham knuckle or 6 oz lean back bacon,
    chopped
4 large tomatoes, skinned and chopped
2 fresh or dried bay leaves
1½ cups chopped potatoes
1 tbsp white-wine vinegar
¼ tsp ground allspice
salt and pepper
scallions or chopped fresh parsley to garnish

1 Put the lentils and stock or water in a saucepan and let soak for 1–2 hours.

2 Add the onions, garlic, carrots, ham knuckle or bacon, tomatoes, bay leaves, and seasoning.

3 Bring to a boil, then cover and simmer for about 1 hour until the lentils are tender.

4 Add the potatoes and continue to simmer for about 20 minutes until the potatoes and ham are tender.

5 Discard the bay leaves. Remove the knuckle and chop about ¾ cup of the meat and reserve. If liked, press half the soup through a strainer or blend in a food processor or blender until smooth. Return to the pan with the rest of the soup.

6 Adjust the seasoning and add the vinegar and allspice and the reserved chopped ham. Simmer for 5–10 minutes longer. Serve sprinkled liberally with scallions or chopped parsley.

VARIATION

For a smoother consistency, press all of the soup through a strainer or blend in a food processor or blender in step 5, before adding the meat.

STEP 5

SPLIT PEA & HAM SOUP

Either yellow or green split peas can be used for this recipe but both types must be well rinsed and soaked overnight before use. Any sort of ham bone can be used, but a small knuckle is very economical.

STEP 2

SERVES 6

1½ cups dried yellow split peas
7½ cups water
2 onions, chopped finely
1 small turnip, chopped finely
2 carrots, chopped finely
2–4 celery stalks, chopped finely
1 ham knuckle
1 Bouquet Garni (see page 78)
½ tsp dried thyme
½ tsp ground ginger
1 tbsp white-wine vinegar
salt and pepper

1 Thoroughly wash the dried peas under cold running water, then place in a bowl with half the water and leave to soak overnight.

2 Put the soaked peas and their liquid, the remaining water, the onions, turnip, carrots, and celery into a large saucepan, then add the ham knuckle, bouquet garni, dried thyme, and ginger. Bring slowly to a boil.

3 Remove any foam from the surface of the soup, cover the pan, and simmer for 2–2½ hours until the peas are very tender.

4 Remove the ham knuckle and bouquet garni. Strip about ¼–1 cup of meat from the knuckle and chop it finely.

5 Add the chopped ham and vinegar to the soup and season to taste.

6 Bring back to a boil, then lower the heat and simmer for 3–4 minutes. Serve.

STEP 3

STEP 4

VARIATION

If preferred, this soup can be strained or blended in a food processor or blender until smooth. You can add more or less any type of vegetable depending on what is available. Leeks, celery root, or chopped or canned tomatoes are particularly good.

STEP 5

MULLIGATAWNY SOUP

This warming soup, which is based on Madras curry, became popular with British army officers in India at the beginning of the century, when they carried flasks of it into the cold hills for sustenance.

STEP 1

STEP 3

STEP 4

STEP 5

SERVES 4–6

3 tbsp butter or margarine
1 large onion, chopped
2 carrots, chopped
2–3 celery stalks, chopped
1 eating apple, peeled, cored, and chopped
1 tbsp all-purpose flour
1–2 tsp Madras curry powder
1–2 tsp curry paste
$^1/_2$ tsp ground coriander
$5^1/_2$ cups Beef, Chicken or Vegetable Stock (see pages 76–8)
8-oz can crushed tomatoes
$^1/_2$ cup cooked long-grain rice (optional)
$^1/_3$–$^1/_2$ cup very finely chopped cooked chicken, beef or lamb
salt and pepper

1 Melt the butter or margarine in a large saucepan and fry the onion, carrots, celery, and apple, stirring occasionally, until just soft and lightly browned.

2 Stir in the flour, curry powder, curry paste, and coriander and cook for a minute or so, stirring all the time.

3 Gradually add the stock and bring to a boil, stirring constantly.

Add the tomatoes and plenty of seasoning, cover the pan, and simmer for about 45 minutes until the vegetables and apple are very tender.

4 Cool the soup a little, then press it through a strainer or blend in a food processor or blender until smooth. Pour into a clean pan.

5 Add the rice, if using, and the chicken or meat. Adjust the seasoning and bring to the boil then simmer for 5 minutes.

6 Serve the soup in warmed bowls.

FREEZING

This soup may be frozen for a maximum of 1 month; the spices may cause it to taste musty if stored for any longer.

MAKING SOUPS & BROTHS

ACCOMPANIMENTS
The obvious accompaniment to a soup or broth is fresh crusty bread such as French, Italian, rye, oatmeal, or mixed grain. Breads flavored with olives, onions, walnuts, mixed seeds, and cheese, and rolls of all shapes and sizes can also be served. The important thing is that the bread is very fresh, and it is often best served warm.

Garlic bread
Cut a long French stick in half, or use two short French sticks or an Italian (rather fatter loaf). Blend about ½ cup butter with 3–6 crushed garlic cloves. Cut the loaf into slanting slices about 1 in. thick, leaving a hinge on the base crust. Spread each slice with the butter, reshape the loaf, and wrap tightly in foil. Before serving, place in a preheated oven at 400–425°F for about 20 minutes until hot and crisp. Fold back the foil and allow each guest to pull off slices as required.

VARIATIONS
Herb bread
Mix 3 tablespoons chopped fresh herbs (one type or mixed) or 1½ tablespoons dried herbs with the butter.

Anchovy bread
Mix a well drained and finely chopped can of anchovy fillets or 2½ oz anchovy paste with the butter.

Making soup is one of the most satisfying cooking techniques: it is simple to do, yet always produces tasty results. A wide range of ingredients can be used and it is easy to make substitutions when certain ingredients are not available. Soup making is also an excellent way of using up leftovers, whether the bones or carcass of roast meat or poultry, or cooked meat or vegetables.

STOCKS
The secret of a good soup lies in preparing a very good stock to use for the base, and although there are excellent stock cubes of all flavors readily available, it is homemade stock that puts the edge on any soup.

Stocks can be made in a variety of flavors and colors. A light or white stock requires raw, light-colored bones, preferably veal, but these are not always available, so lamb and beef bones may also be used. For a darker stock it is necessary to use beef bones that have been roasted, so they darken. A poultry stock using chicken or turkey bones and carcasses is also light colored, but if you use game carcasses, the stock will be darker and much stronger in flavor. To make fish stock, use fish heads, tails, and trimmings, including the skin. You can buy fish trimmings from a fishmonger.

Bones alone are not sufficient for a good stock; you will also need a couple of chopped or sliced onions and two or three root vegetables, such as carrots, rutabaga, or turnips, but avoid potatoes because they break up and make the stock cloudy. Celery and leeks can also be included. Flavorings such as one or two bay leaves may be added (use fresh ones if they are available as they have a better flavor than dried) or a Bouquet Garni (see page 78), but do not add any seasoning. It should be added when the soup is made and depends on the other ingredients.

Put all the ingredients in a large saucepan, with the measured amount of water or enough to cover the contents of the pan: usually 1¾–2½ quarts. Once the water comes to a boil it is essential to remove the foam that forms on the surface, using a perforated spoon, before covering the pan and simmering for the recommended time. Fish stock should be simmered for only 30 minutes, as overcooking will give it a slightly bitter taste. Vegetable stock needs one hour's cooking, but all other kinds of stock need at least 2 hours, and for beef stock 3–4 hours is best. A pressure cooker is an ideal appliance for cutting down on the time it takes to make stock: simply follow the manufacturer's directions.

General-purpose stock
about 2 lb bones from a cooked joint or raw chopped beef, lamb, or veal bones
2 onions, studded with 6 cloves, or sliced or chopped coarsely
2 carrots, sliced
1 leek, sliced
1–2 celery stalks, sliced
1 Bouquet Garni (see page 78)
about 2½ quarts water

Chop or break up the bones and place in a large saucepan with the other ingredients. Bring to a boil, removing foam from the surface with a perforated spoon. Cover and simmer for 3–4 hours.

Strain the stock and leave to cool. Remove any fat from the surface and chill. If stored for more than 24 hours, the stock must be boiled every day, cooled quickly, and chilled again. The stock may be frozen for up to 2 months; place in a large plastic bag and seal, leaving at least 1 in. of headspace to allow for expansion.

White stock

Make as above but use a knuckle of veal, veal bones, or raw lamb or beef bones and add a sliced lemon to the stockpot.

Brown beef stock

Use chopped marrow bones with a few strips of shin of beef if possible. Put in a roasting pan and roast in a preheated oven at 450°F for 30–50 minutes until browned. Transfer to a large saucepan, add the vegetables and water, then continue as before.

Chicken, turkey or game stock

1 raw or cooked carcass of a chicken, turkey, or 1–2 game birds
giblets, if available
2 onions, sliced or chopped
2 carrots, sliced
2–4 celery stalks, sliced
1 Bouquet Garni (see page 78) or 2–3 fresh or dried bay leaves

Break up the carcasses and place in a large saucepan with the remaining ingredients. Add enough water to cover. Bring to a boil and remove any foam, then simmer for 2–3 hours. It is a good idea to give the bones a good stir and break them up a little during cooking. Strain, cool, and store as for general-purpose stock.

Fish stock

1 head of a cod or salmon, or so on, plus the trimmings, skin, and bones, or just the trimmings, skin, and bones
1–2 onions, sliced
1 carrot, sliced
1–2 celery stalks, sliced
good squeeze of lemon juice
1 Bouquet Garni (see page 78) or 2 fresh or dried bay leaves

Wash the fish head and trimmings and place in a saucepan. Cover with water and bring to a boil. Remove any foam with a perforated spoon, then add the remaining ingredients. Cover and simmer for about 30 minutes. Strain and cool. Store in the refrigerator and use within 2 days.

Vegetable stock

To make vegetable stock you need a good selection of green and root vegetables, including onion and, if possible, leeks, but not potatoes. Take care when using very strongly flavored vegetables such as celery root and Jersusalem artichokes, as they will overpower the others. Coarsely

Curry bread

Mix 2–3 teaspoons curry powder with the butter.

Poppadoms

These are ideal fried or broiled and served with curry-flavored soups, such as Mulligatawny Soup (see page 74) or, indeed, any soup. Use either plain or flavored poppadoms, and cut or break into smaller pieces before frying. They can be prepared earlier in the day.

Biscuits

Warm biscuits with savory flavors and toppings make excellent accompaniments to soups, especially when freshly made and served warm.

2 cups self-rising flour
¼ cup butter or margarine
1 egg, beaten
good squeeze lemon juice
about ⅓ cup milk
salt and pepper

Sift together the flour and seasoning, then rub in the butter or margarine until the mixture resembles fine bread crumbs. Add the egg and lemon juice and enough milk to bind to a soft dough. Turn out onto a floured counter and flatten out with your hands to about ¾ in. thick. Either shape into a bar or cut into circles squares, triangles, or fingers and place on a floured cookie sheet. Dredge with flour or glaze with beaten egg or milk. Sprinkle with sesame, pumpkin, sunflower, or poppy seeds, finely chopped or flaked nuts, grated cheese, crumbled crisp bacon, or steel-cut oats, if liked. Bake in a preheated oven at 425°F for about 15 minutes for individual biscuits, or 20–25 minutes for a biscuit bar. Cool slightly on a wire rack before serving.

VARIATIONS

Herb biscuits
Add 2 tbsp chopped fresh herbs (one type or mixed) or 2 teaspoons dried herbs.

Cheese biscuits
¼ cup grated blue or sharp Cheddar cheese or 3 tablespoons grated Parmesan cheese.

Anchovy biscuits
Add a drained and very finely chopped can of anchovy fillets

Nut biscuits
Add scant ½ cup finely chopped walnuts, pecan nuts, hazelnuts, or almonds

Bacon biscuits
Add scant ½ cup very finely chopped lean bacon.

chop about 1 lb mixed vegetables, cover generously with water, cover, and simmer for about 1 hour. Strain and keep in the refrigerator for up to 24 hours.

BOUQUET GARNI

A bouquet garni is simply a bunch of herbs which is used to give flavor to stocks, soups, stews, and sauces. The herbs can be made into a small bunch and tied with string, or they can be tied in cheesecloth, which is essential if you include dried herbs, cloves or peppercorns, as they should be easy to remove before serving. Herbs such as rosemary, sage, fennel, and dill can be used but remember that these are very strongly flavored and must blend with the dish to be made.

Traditional bouquet garni

1 fresh or dried bay leaf
few sprigs of fresh parsley
few sprigs of fresh thyme

Tie the herbs together with a piece of string or thread.

Dried bouquet garni

1 dried bay leaf
good pinch of Italian seasoning or any one dried herb
good pinch of dried parsley
8–10 black peppercorns
2–4 cloves
1 garlic clove (optional)

Put all the ingredients in a small square

of cheesecloth and secure with string or thread, leaving a long tail so it can be tied to the handle of the pan for easy removal.

GARNISHES

The appearance of a soup can be greatly enhanced by a suitable garnish. The simplest garnishes are chopped herbs, which can be added to the soup itself and sprinkled on top. The type of herb should complement the flavor of the soup, but parsley and chives blend with almost any soup. Whole leaves and small sprigs of herbs, such as mint, oregano, fennel, and dill can also be used as they will float on the surface. Dried herbs are not an attractive garnish but can be added to the soup during cooking.

Lemon, orange, or lime rind can be grated or cut into fine strips. Coarsely grated rind or strips should be blanched in boiling water for 2–3 minutes if they are to be eaten. With care, they too will float on the surface. Very thin slices of lemon or lime can also be floated on top of soups, particularly chilled ones, such as Gazpacho (see page 8).

Vegetables, such as carrots, turnips, rutabaga and celery root can be coarsely grated into a soup just before serving, to add color and texture. Leeks can be cut into very thin rings and used either raw or blanched. Fried, thin onion rings and blanched or lightly fried, thinly sliced mushrooms can also be used as garnishes. Coarsely grated cheese such as Cheddar, red, Swis, and blue are good sprinkled over soups. Very crisply fried or broiled bacon can be crumbled and used as a garnish.

Croutons

These can be served separately, to be sprinkled on the soup by your guests or placed on each portion before serving.

Toasted croutons

Toast slices of bread and cut into cubes, triangles, or other shapes while hot. Cocktail cutters or aspic cutters will allow you to cut out a variety of shapes. Allow to cool. These can be stored in an airtight container for two to three days.

Fried croutons

These are best cut into shapes before cooking. Fry in shallow oil for a few minutes, turning until golden on both sides. The oil must be hot, but take care as the bread will brown very quickly. Drain on paper towels. Croûtons may be dipped in chopped herbs, paprika, or chopped hard-cooked egg.

Garlic croutons

Make as for fried croutons, adding 3–4 crushed garlic cloves to the oil.

Pastry crescents

Crescents or other shapes can be cut from puff or basic piecrust dough, glazed with beaten egg or milk, and topped with sesame seeds, poppy seeds, or finely chopped nuts. Bake in a preheated oven at 400°F for about 10 minutes until golden brown.

Garnishes for consommé

This clear soup is traditionally served with a garnish of freshly cooked tiny pasta shapes, noodles, rice, lightly cooked diced or julienne of vegetables, or thinly sliced mushrooms. Or make a one-egg omelet, drain thoroughly on paper towels, then cut into strips or shapes.

THICKENING SOUPS

A variety of thickening agents can be used, depending on the type of soup.

Cream

To prevent curdling, put the cream in a bowl and add a little of the hot soup, then stir into the soup. Reheat but don't let the soup boil.

Flour and cornflour (cornstarch)

Blend all-purpose flour or cornstarch with a little cold milk or water and add a little of the hot soup, then whisk back into the soup. Simmer for a few minutes, until the soup thickens.

Beurre manié

Blend equal quantities of sifted all-purpose flour and butter or margarine, then whisk small amounts into the soup, until blended. Simmer for 3–4 minutes.

Egg yolks

Blend egg yolks with a little milk or cream, then add a little of the soup. Strain the mixture into the soup, off the heat, whisking thoroughly. Reheat the soup but do not let it boil.

Cheese & anchovy twists

Unroll a package of thawed puff pastry dough and cut in half lengthwise. Spread one piece evenly with anchovy paste, then cover evenly with about 1 1/2 cups finely grated Gouda or Swiss cheese. A little grated Parmesan cheese may also be sprinkled over.

Place the other piece of dough on top and press together firmly. Using a sharp knife and ruler, cut into strips about 1/2 in. wide. If liked, brush with beaten egg or milk. Give each strip two twists and place on a greased cookie sheet. Shape the ends into points and make sure they are evenly shaped all over.

Bake in a preheated oven at 400°F for about 15 minutes until well puffed up and golden brown. Serve warm or cold. The twists can be frozen for up to 1 month.

INDEX

Accompaniments, 76–9
anchovies: anchovy biscuits 78
 anchovy bread, 76
 cheese and anchovy twists, 79
apple and apricot soup, spiced, 15
apricots: spiced apple and apricot soup,
 15
artichokes, Jerusalem see Jerusalem
 artichokes
avocado and mint soup, 12

Bacon biscuits, 78
barley: Scotch broth, 68
beans: red bean chowder, 58
beef: brown beef stock, 77
 consommé, 66
 mulligatawny soup, 74
 red bean chowder, 58
beet: bortsch, 22
 creamed beet soup, 22
bell peppers: gazpacho, 8
 shrimp gumbo, 42
beurre manié, thickening soups, 79
biscuits, 77–8
 anchovy, 78
 bacon, 78
 cheese, 78
 herb, 78
 nut, 78
bisque, salmon, 46
bortsch, 22
bouillabaisse, 36
bouquet garni, 78
bread: anchovy bread, 76
 croutons, 79
 curry bread, 77
 garlic bread, 76
 herb bread, 76
 minted garlic bread, 12
broths: gardener's broth, 32
 Scotch broth, 68
brown beef stock, 77
Brussels sprouts: gardener's broth, 32

Carrots: creamed carrot and cumin
 soup, 27
 hollandaise-oat chowder, 50
celery: hollandaise oatmeal chowder,
 50
cheese: anchovy biscuits 78
 cheese and anchovy twists, 79
 cheese biscuits 78
 French onion soup, 20
 hollandaise-oat chowder, 50
chestnuts: chicken and chestnut soup,
 62
chicken: chicken and chestnut soup, 62
 chicken stock, 77
 cock-a-leekie soup, 55

mulligatawny soup, 74
chilled soups, 7–16
chowders, 49–58
 cock-a-leekie soup, 55
 curried cod chowder, 52
 hollandaise-oat chowder, 50
 red bean chowder, 58
 sage and onion chowder, 56
cock-a-leekie soup, 55
cod chowder, curried, 52
consommé, 66
 garnishes for, 79
cornstarch, thickening soups, 79
crab, 41
 partan bree, 41
cream, thickening soups, 79
cream of artichoke soup, 28
creamed carrot and cumin soup, 27
creamed parsnip and tarragon soup, 24
creamed pheasant soup, 64
croutons, 79
cumin: creamed carrot and cumin
 soup, 27
curries: curried cod chowder, 52
 curried shrimp soup, 16
 curry bread, 77
 mulligatawny soup, 74

Dried bouquet garni, 78

Egg yolks, thickening soups, 79

Fish soups, 35–46
fish stock, 77
flour, thickening soups, 79
French onion soup, 20
fried croutons, 79
fruit soups, 15
 spiced apple and apricot soup, 15

Game stock, 77
gardener's broth, 32
garlic: garlic bread, 76
 garlic croutons, 79
 minted garlic bread, 12
garnishes, 78–9
gazpacho, 8
general-purpose stock, 76–7
green beans: gardener's broth, 32
gumbo, shrimp, 42

Haddock: curried cod chowder, 52
 smoky haddock soup, 44
ham: lentil and ham soup, 70
 split pea and ham soup, 73
herbs: bouquet garni, 78
 garnishes, 78
 herb biscuits, 78
 herb bread, 76

hollandaise-oat chowder, 50

Jerusalem artichokes: cream of
 Jerusalem artichoke soup, 28

Lamb: Scotch broth, 68
leeks: cock-a-leekie soup, 55
 hollandaise-oat chowder, 50
 vichyssoise, 10
lemon, garnishes, 78
lentil and ham soup, 70

Meat soups, 61, 66–74
mint: avocado and mint soup, 12
 minted garlic bread, 12
moules marinière, 38
mulligatawny soup, 74
mushrooms: creamed pheasant soup,
 64
mussels, 38
 moules marinière, 38

Nut biscuits, 78

Oats: chowder, hollandaise, 50
okra: shrimp gumbo, 42
onions: French onion soup, 20
 sage and onion chowder, 56

Parsnip and tarragon soup, creamed,
 24
partan bree, 41
pastry crescents, 79
pearl barley: Scotch broth, 68
peas: gardener's broth, 32
 split pea and ham soup, 73
pheasant soup, creamed, 64
poppadoms, 77
potatoes: lentil and bacon soup, 70
 sage and onion chowder, 56
 Scotch broth, 68
 smoky haddock soup, 44
 vichyssoise, 10
poultry soups, 61–4
prunes: cock-a-leekie soup, 55
pumpkin soup, 30

Red bean chowder, 58
rice: curried cod chowder, 52
 mulligatawny soup, 74
 partan bree, 41
 shrimp gumbo, 42

Sage and onion chowder, 56
salmon bisque, 46
Scotch broth, 68
shrimp: curried shrimp soup, 16
 shrimp gumbo, 42
smoky haddock soup, 44

spiced apple and apricot soup, 15
split pea and ham soup, 73
stocks, 76–8
 brown beef, 77
 chicken, 77
 fish, 77
 game, 77
 general-purpose, 76–7
 turkey, 77
 vegetable, 77–8
 white, 77

Tarragon: creamed parsnip and
 tarragon soup, 24
thickening soups, 79
toasted croutons, 79
tomatoes: bouillabaisse, 36
 curried cod chowder, 52
 gazpacho, 8
 lentil and bacon soup, 70
 mulligatawny soup, 74
turkey stock, 77
turnips: hollandaise-oat chowder, 50

Vegetable garnishes, 78
vegetable soups, 19–32
vegetable stock, 77–8
vichyssoise, 10

Walnuts: nut biscuits 78
white stock, 77